Haunted

D1650126

A play

Eric Chappell

Samuel French — London
New York - Toronto - Hollywood

HAUNTED

First performed at the Theatre Royal, Windsor on the 13th September 1994 with the following cast:

Nigel Burke	Keith Barron
Mary Burke	Maureen Beattie
Potter	Sam Kelly
Julia Phillips	Joanna Van Gyseghem
Lord Byron	James Barron
Turner Gould	Peter Blythe

Directed by Mark Piper
Designed by Alexander McPherson
Lighting by Mark Doubleday
Technical Adviser Paul Kieve

CHARACTERS

Nigel Burke, 40s
Mary Burke, 40s
Potter
Julia Phillips, late 30s
Lord Byron, 36
Turner Gould, mid-40s

The action takes place in Nigel's study in the Burkes'
home in the country

ACT I

ACT II

Time — the present

AUTHOR'S NOTE

The "magic" element in the play will be dependent on the
attitude of the director. In the original production panels
and trapdoors were used to make Byron's appearances
more "supernatural", but simply fading to black, with
dramatic sound effects, would serve equally well. (In fact,
the text does make some fun of Byron's first faltering
steps as a ghost.)

Also by Eric Chappell, published by
Samuel French Ltd

Natural Causes

ACT I

Nigel Burke's study. Evening. Late October

The study is a long, rambling room converted from an old milking parlour and almost independent of the cottage to which it is attached. It is timbered and plastered, with a low window running almost its length

A door, US, leads into the large, overgrown garden; another, R, leads into the hall. There is a large desk by the window with a high-backed executive chair behind it. Among the papers on the desk are a number of bottles of tablets, a torch, a bottle of wine and some glasses, and a table lamp. There are pictures of Lord Byron on the walls and a bust of him on the desk. The design on the chintz curtains at the window is picked up in the sofa and easy chairs

When the CURTAIN rises, the executive chair is facing the window. A low musical sound comes from the chair. It spins round to reveal Nigel Burke, a man in his thirties. He is turning two coloured metal balls over in his hands. These are making the musical sound. He sighs, puts the balls away and takes a drink from a glass of red wine. He glances at the bust of Byron

Nigel It's all right for you, George. You're dead. Dead at thirty-six and never knew failure. Well, I don't know what death's like but it must be an improvement on this ...

The low whining of a dog comes from the garden

(*Frowning*) There it goes again ... (*He drains his glass, picks up a torch and crosses to the garden door. He peers out and shines the torch*)

The whining sound turns into a growl

Nigel closes the door abruptly, returns to the desk and pours himself another large glass of wine. Then he stares out of the window

Mary (*off*) Nigel ...

Nigel You didn't take your tablets this morning.

Mary enters. She is about Nigel's age but looks younger. She is slim, attractive and is wearing a dark tracksuit

Mary You didn't take your tablets this morning.

Nigel I'll take twice as many tonight.

Mary It doesn't work like that. Your body can only take so much.

Nigel You're telling me that? I know my body can only take so much and my God it's taken it. I feel terrible.

Mary Then stop complaining and take your tablets. (*She lays out the pills*)

Nigel What am I taking?

Mary Multi-vitamins, cod-liver oil ... arthritis ... and the little pink one?

Nigel What's the little pink one?

Mary (*quietly*) Valium.

Nigel Valium. Are you trying to drug me?

Mary No, but you're much nicer after Valium. Although I don't think you should take it with red wine.

Nigel I don't think I should take any of them — they don't work.

Mary Of course they work.

Nigel Then why do I feel terrible?

Mary You'd feel worse if you didn't take them.

Nigel Mary, I feel nervous, tense and tired and I can't get out of the bath. How could I feel worse?

Mary Of course you can get out of the bath. If you couldn't get out of the bath you wouldn't be sitting here.

Nigel I've had to devise an entirely new method of getting out of the bath and even then it's a struggle. If things get much worse I shall either have to fill it to the top and float over the edge or use a block and tackle. (*He takes up the metal balls and begins turning them furiously in his hands*)

Mary I take it you've nothing for me to read?

Nigel You know I don't write in the evenings.

Mary Then what do you do in here? Talk to Lord Byron?

Nigel (*uneasily*) Don't be silly, Mary. I read what I've written in the morning.

Mary Then let me read that.

Nigel I haven't written anything.

Mary So you can't write in the mornings either?

Nigel You know I can only work if I get up at six o'clock.

Mary Then why don't you get up at six o'clock?

Nigel I'm too tired.

Mary Nigel, you haven't written a word in three months.

Nigel That shows how tired I am.

Mary How can you be tired? You don't do anything except juggle those bloody balls — which obviously aren't working.

Nigel Neither are the tablets.

Mary You should make a start; your horoscope's good.

Nigel Is it? So one twelfth of the world's population can look forward to a good month, can they? Well, I hope we're not all going to make a journey — the trains are going to be rather crowded.

Mary Incidentally, you share a birthday with the Prime Minister.

Nigel That doesn't exactly fill me with confidence, Mary.

Mary I wish you'd pull yourself together.

Nigel Pull myself together. That's the worst advice you can give to someone who's in the middle of a nervous breakdown.

Mary You're not having a nervous breakdown.

Nigel My father had a nervous breakdown.

Mary That's no reason why you should have one.

Nigel He thought he was being pursued by little green men, four foot tall, one eye in the middle and covered in slime. He thought they'd landed in the garden and that they were trying to immobilize him with ray guns.

Mary Why should they have wanted to do that?

Nigel They wanted to take him back with them — as a perfect physical specimen.

Mary He wasn't a perfect physical specimen; he was out of condition and he always looked strange, even before he went bonkers.

Nigel I know but if you were four foot tall and covered in slime he wouldn't look too bad. Anyway, he went to bed every night wrapped in cooking foil to deflect the rays. He looked like an oven-ready chicken.

Mary Nigel, you're not having a nervous breakdown but I shall if you don't improve. You're living like a recluse.

Nigel I am a recluse.

Mary (*hesitating*) Not quite. There's someone coming to see you tonight.

Nigel (*alarmed*) Who?

Mary Julia Phillips. She phoned earlier. She said you met at a writers' weekend in Harrogate last year. You shared the platform.

Nigel Yes, I remember. Why does she want to see me? I hate her.

Mary Why?

Nigel Because she's horrible. I told you about her. I told you how much I hated her. Why did you have to say yes?

Mary Why didn't you answer the phone?

Nigel You know I don't answer the phone.

Mary Why not?

Nigel I have this fear of bad news.

Mary Well, now you've got it: she's coming. And since you're almost agoraphobic it's your only way of meeting people.

Nigel I also have a phobia about meeting people.

Mary You have a phobia about most things. I was listing them the other day. I got to forty-nine before the pencil broke. The doctor told you to measure your fears on a scale of one to ten and attempt nothing over five. Do you know what your average is between one and ten? Eleven.

Nigel I can't help it. I'm allergic to the twentieth century. I should be in a plastic bubble.

Mary Perhaps you can hang on until the twenty-first — you haven't long to go.

Nigel Think that's going to be any better? And you ask Julia Phillips, a woman I hate and detest, to come here and see me. I won't see her.

Mary (*shrewdly*) Did her talk go better than yours?

Nigel Of course it did. The audience was full of lesbians; they follow her around.

Mary (*alarmed*) Nigel, don't say that to her; she's an ardent feminist.

Nigel I'm not saying anything to her.

Mary crosses to the hall door

Where are you going?

Mary To have a shower.

Nigel You can't.

Mary Nigel, I've been helping the aged all day. I've had a run. I have a parish council meeting this evening. I need a shower.

Nigel You mean you're going to leave me to answer the door?

Mary You'll have to start sometime, Nigel. When Mr Harris called the other day he said he thought you were hiding under the stairs.

Nigel I've told you — I don't like visitors.

Mary He's not a visitor. He's a neighbour.

Nigel (*after a pause*) Does he have a dog?

Mary A dog? No. Why?

Nigel (*looking out of the window*) There was a dog in the garden just now. Must have wandered in from the churchyard.

Mary I didn't see it.

Nigel It was whining ... a few minutes ago.

Mary What did it look like?

Nigel Large — black and white, I think — with a sort of twisted tail ...

Mary I don't know anyone with a dog like that.

Nigel Are you suggesting I'm seeing things?

Mary Of course not. (*She opens the door*)

Nigel Where are you going?

Mary (*sighing*) To have a shower. I'll be as quick as I can. (*She returns and kisses him lightly*) Poor Nigel — what would you do without me?

She exits

Nigel (*grimly*) I don't know, Mary. (*He turns to the bust of Byron*) You wouldn't like Julia Phillips, George. She has this whinnying laugh — this careless toss of the head — a little break in her voice and the most self-deprecating smile you've ever seen. Mind you, she has a lot to be self-deprecating about. She's written the same book for twenty years — a woman in a mid-life crisis chasing someone who looks like her father ——

There is the faint sound of a doorbell

(*Breaking off and listening intently*) My God! She's here. (*He crosses and listens at the hall door*)

There is the sound of footsteps on the gravel outside, then a tap on the garden door

Nigel crouches behind the desk

Potter enters. He is a nondescript little man in a plain raincoat, carrying a Harrods bag

Potter discovers Nigel behind the desk. Their eyes meet

Nigel (*rising*) Oh. Hallo.
Potter Hallo.
Nigel My pen ... rolled under the desk.
Potter I thought there was someone here; that's why I persisted. I knew you'd want to see me.
Nigel Did you? (*He hesitates*) Well, normally I would but I'm afraid I'm somewhat drained. Writing for six hours. Don't let anyone tell you it gets easier, Mr ... er —— ?
Potter Potter. I'm sure it doesn't, Mr Burke, and I wouldn't have disturbed you but you did say if there was anything at all ...
Nigel (*staring*) Did I?
Potter You were most insistent.
Nigel Oh. Was it Harrogate? If it's a script ... (*He shuffles the papers on his desk*) I really haven't had time but as soon ...
Potter I'm not a writer, Mr Burke.
Nigel Then I doubt if we've met. You see, I'm agoraphobic — I rarely go out.
Potter You really don't remember me, do you?
Nigel No. I'm sorry.
Potter That's all right. No reason why you should. It was a long time ago and I'm not a memorable person, easily forgotten.

Nigel No, I'm sure you're not, Mr ... er ——

Potter Potter. Oh, yes, totally forgettable. My own mother says that when I enter a room it's as if someone has switched off a light.

Nigel I'm sure she didn't mean ——

Potter Of course it may be something to do with my height ... (*He watches Nigel closely*) I am below medium height, Mr Burke ...

Nigel I hadn't noticed. I think I do remember you now, Mr Potter.

Potter Let me jog your memory. Newstead. Two years ago. You gave me your card.

Nigel Newstead?

Potter The Abbey. I was the guide. Potter.

Nigel Yes — now I remember.

Potter We had a long talk about his lordship.

Nigel He is a particular interest of mine, as you can see.

Potter You said you felt this affinity.

Nigel I do.

Potter And we discussed ... (*he pauses slightly*) memorabilia ...

Nigel Memorabilia?

Potter You were interested in acquiring ... memorabilia.

Nigel Well, yes.

Potter I do have some ... memorabilia which is unusual, I might even say unique. (*He moves the bag between them but keeps his hand on it*) A collector would give his soul for what I have here, Mr Burke.

Nigel A Harrods bag. That's unusual.

Potter Yes. I find it makes the right impression. People may forget me but they certainly don't forget a Harrods bag. Don't you agree?

Nigel Yes. Is it something from the Abbey?

Potter Certainly not. That's a sacred trust. No — this came from Hucknall. Does Hucknall mean anything to you?

Nigel Yes, that's where Byron's buried.

Potter Precisely. Now, let me ask you another question. What happened in the church of St Mary Magdalene on June the fifteenth nineteen thirty-eight — at dead of night?

Nigel Didn't they break into the tomb?

Potter They entered the tomb by Act of Parliament.

Nigel Yes. I never understood why.

Potter Some say it was for treasure but I think it was curiosity. They wanted to see Byron and when they did see him they found him as handsome as the day he died — over a hundred years before. How do you account for that?

Nigel I can't.

Potter (*lowering his voice*) They say the genitalia were magnificent. What a man, Mr Burke.

Nigel Hadn't someone cut his foot off?

Potter Yes. And his brains and heart were in a jar but apart from that: perfect.

Nigel Why are you telling me this story, Mr Potter?

Potter Because there were a number of people in the church that night and one of them was an apprentice stonemason named Arnold Fisher. He was one of the first into the tomb and the last one out before it was sealed. The family I represent is called Fisher. Now do you begin to understand?

Nigel (*leaning forward*) He took something.

Potter He did indeed. Now, Arnold Fisher died many years ago and left his personal effects in a trunk to his brother William who died recently. The family opened the trunk and found something that both surprised and shocked them. Knowing my interest in the subject they asked me to evaluate it and represent them in the matter. (*He pushes the bag towards Nigel*) This was in the trunk ...

Nigel reaches out; Potter stays his hand

Are you of a nervous disposition, Mr Burke?

Nigel Why? (*Nervously*) It's not his foot, is it?

Potter No, but it may make your flesh creep a little ... (*He takes a large goblet made from bone and silver from the bag*)

Nigel It's a goblet.

Potter The skull goblet. The one he drank from, Mr Burke.

Nigel My God! I thought it had been buried in the Abbey grounds.

Potter Not so.

Nigel But this could be worth a fortune. Why bring it to me?

Potter Why not? We could hardly take it to Sotheby's. Questions would be asked, and the family don't wish to be accused of grave robbing. No, a private collector, that's the answer. I'm sure you'll give us a fair price.

Nigel (*hesitating*) I'll have to think about it, Mr Potter.

Potter Of course. No hurry. I'll leave it here.

Nigel Leave it?

Potter Yes, I'm staying with friends. They have children. I think it would be safer.

Nigel Are you sure?

Potter Yes. (*He pauses*) Although ... I wouldn't drink from it, Mr Burke ...

Nigel Why not?

Potter (*slowly*) It has been a long time; it may have deteriorated. I don't think it would be wise ... or even proper. I hope you don't think that's a drawback?

Nigel No. We do have glasses, Mr Potter.

Nigel escorts Potter to the door

Oh, by the way — did you bring a dog?

Potter (*stopping, staring*) A dog? What sort of dog?

Nigel A sort of broad, muscular dog, black and white.

Potter You mean ... medium height, broad-chested, loose-haired sort of dog, with a twisted tail?

Nigel Yes. Is it yours?

Potter No.

Nigel But you've seen it?

Potter No.

Nigel Then I don't understand.

Potter It's just that you've described the old Newfoundland.

Nigel What?

Potter Byron's dog. Bosun. Buried at Newstead. Went mad in eighteen-o-eight. No one knew why. Good-night, Mr Burke.

Potter exits into the garden

Nigel returns to his desk and places the goblet by the bust of Byron

Nigel Well, George, I bet you didn't expect to see him again. You must have had some great nights together. Well, you did, I don't know about him. (*He considers and then pours wine into the goblet and studies it*) My word. You wouldn't have needed many of these to become paralytic ...

There is a loud crash against the garden door followed by a loud scratching sound. The door shakes on its hinges

Nigel starts, almost dropping the goblet. Silence. He takes up the torch and a walking stick from the corner of the room and steps nervously out into the garden, disappearing out of sight

There is the sound of steps on the gravel path

Julia Phillips appears at the open door and enters diffidently, carrying a manuscript. She is tall, dark-haired and a little older than Nigel

A moment later Nigel backs into the room still holding the walking stick raised

Julia Nigel?

Nigel (*whirling around*) Julia!

Julia I'm sorry. Did I surprise you?

Nigel No ... that's all right.

Julia Only I saw this man leaving and he suggested I used the study door.

Nigel That must have been Potter.
Julia I think he was looking for his dog.
Nigel What?
Julia He asked me if I'd seen a dog.
Nigel Oh. (*He looks nervously out of the window*)

During the following, Julia sits down

Julia I hope you don't mind me calling?
Nigel Not at all. When my wife told me I was so excited.
Julia I'm afraid I can't stay long.
Nigel How disappointing. Can I get you a drink?
Julia No, I'm driving. I'm on my way to Nottingham. But since I was passing I thought I'd hold you to your promise.
Nigel Promise? What promise?
Julia To read my play.
Nigel But you write novels.
Julia But now I've written a play and I've sent it to the Royal Court but apparently they can take sixteen weeks and I wanted an opinion.
Nigel (*hesitating*) Well, I'm not what one would call a serious dramatist, Julia. (*Worriedly*) Is it about a woman in a mid-life crisis?
Julia How did you guess?
Nigel Well, your books do have that recurring theme.
Julia That sounds boring.

Nigel almost drinks from the goblet, realizes in time and moves to his glass

Nigel No. There's nothing wrong with a recurring theme. Some writers write the same play with different words, other writers write different plays with the same words; it's as broad as it's long. And we should all write about what we know: and if it's mid-life crisis and incest, why not?
Julia Perhaps you don't want to read it?
Nigel No, I'm sure I shall love it, Julia. (*He takes the play from her gingerly*) I'm sure it will have all that nose wrinkling, head tossing, infectious gaiety of yours.
Julia (*doubtfully*) What?
Nigel I mean I'm sure it's a real woman's play.
Julia I've written it for men too.
Nigel Of course. But I've read your books — and they're good, very good. Particularly those descriptions of the countryside and people's faces and oak-panelled dining-rooms. But I have to say I find some of your men ... shadowy figures.
Julia (*sharply*) Shadowy? You mean like some of your women?

Nigel You find my women shadowy?

Julia Not just me, Nigel — the critics.

Nigel Don't quote the critics to me, Julia. They hate me.

Julia No.

Nigel Yes. Hate me.

Julia Never mind, Nigel. You'll be remembered when they've all been forgotten.

Nigel (*darkly*) Not by me. I won't forget them. I've got all their names — even the ones who passed briefly across the Arts page *en route* from Gardening to Motoring, pausing just long enough to knee me adroitly in the crotch. One day I shall invite them to a dinner at *L'Escargot*, ask them to form a group as though for a photograph and machine-gun the lot of them.

Julia (*giving him a worried glance*) I'm sorry, Nigel. I saw what Carrington did to you in *The Times* after Brighton. It was cruel.

Nigel They only have to see the name Nigel Burke and they reach for the vitriol. (*Broodingly*) I have thought of changing it. Although I would like to retain something of myself. I had thought of an anagram for Nigel Burke. What do you think of Erik Bungle?

Julia (*staring*) Erik Bungle?

Nigel Erik with a k of course.

Julia I think I prefer Nigel Burke.

Nigel (*shrugging*) It was just a thought.

Julia (*rising*) Well, I must be going. I have a meeting with the series editor at Central. I'm pitching an idea.

Nigel Pitching? How American we're all getting. And can we look forward to a little mid-life crisis and incest in the winter schedules?

Julia Er, something like that. Nigel, I hope you don't think I'm encroaching ...

Nigel Encroaching?

Julia With the play. After all, I'm a novelist and this is your field. I'm sure there's enough competition already ...

Nigel Julia, I have to compete with fashionable playwrights who wine and dine with the critics. I have to compete with actors who write and directors who write. I have to compete with Shakespeare, Congreve and Oscar-bloody-Wilde. All the living dead who don't attend rehearsals and don't ask for royalties. There are workshop productions, compilation shows, one man readings and bloody musicals. Do you think I'm worried about one stray lady novelist?

Julia (*her gaze becoming even more disturbed*) Then you don't mind reading it?

Nigel No.

Julia (*crossing to the garden door*) Perhaps I could call for the play on the way back?

Nigel Why not? (*He picks up the play reverently*) I shall read this with
  interest, Julia.
Julia And will you take care of it? It's my last copy.
Nigel I shall guard it with my life — and thank you for letting me see it.
Julia Goodbye.
Nigel Bye.

She exits

*He throws the script casually over his shoulder and watches Julia's depar-
ture through the window. He drinks from the goblet, realizes what he's done
and shudders. He puts the goblet back on the desk*

Mary enters. She picks up the script

Mary Has she gone?
Nigel Yes.
Mary What was she like?
Nigel As repellent as ever.
Mary Did she mention the room?
Nigel What room?
Mary This room.
Nigel Why should she mention the room?
Mary I wondered if she admired it.
Nigel She didn't have time — too busy admiring herself.
Mary She's not like that in her books. She's very observant. She describes
  rooms in great detail.
Nigel That's to fill up the pages and display her superior taste.
Mary No. She's a very sympathetic writer.
Nigel Sympathetic. Then she's nothing like her books. She's about as
  sympathetic as a gin trap.
Mary She's sympathetic on television.
Nigel Of course she is. She's on her best behaviour. But she never smiles with
  her eyes, Mary, they're like steel shutters. (*He pauses*) Do you like her
  books?
Mary She does the sex scenes well.
Nigel Does she? You do surprise me.
Mary Why?
Nigel I found her cold.
Mary She didn't attract you?
Nigel I'd sooner spend the night on an ice floe, Mary.
Mary Well, perhaps you didn't attract her. She has had several affairs.
Nigel Has she? How do you know?
Mary I read this article about her.

Nigel Several. She obviously can't sustain a relationship. Probably something to do with that laugh.

Mary Don't you like her sex scenes?

Nigel I don't read them.

Mary You mean you find them embarrassing.

Nigel No. Why should I?

Mary Well, you don't go in for that sort of thing.

Nigel (*sharply*) Are you suggesting I'm old-fashioned, Mary? There's talk that I'm old-fashioned.

Mary (*hesitating*) No — it's just that you don't get out much. I mean you're over forty and you still can't use the cash dispenser. It does limit you.

Nigel I happen to believe in good taste. I believe you can entertain an audience without exposing them to the sight of a pair of heaving buttocks. If that's old-fashioned I'm proud of it.

Mary Well, comedy isn't really sexy, is it?

Nigel On the contrary, comedy is very sexy. I find humour in a woman very attractive — I just don't come across it very often.

Mary (*picking up the goblet from the desk*) Nigel, where did this come from?

Nigel A man brought it whilst you were in the shower. He wants to sell it.

Mary Why should he think you'd want it?

Nigel It's supposed to be the legendary skull goblet that belonged to Byron. His gardener dug the skull up in the grounds and Byron had it made into a goblet.

Mary Nigel —that's weird.

Nigel Oh, I don't know. Waste not, want not.

Mary What would you do with it?

Nigel I thought I'd keep it in the drinks cabinet.

Mary You're not going to drink from it?

Nigel Why not? Byron did.

Mary That's gruesome.

Nigel What? To put my lips where Byron once placed his? Think of it, Mary.

Mary I am doing. You wouldn't.

Nigel Why not?

Mary For one thing you're not Byron. I've never understood your fascination for him. He was everything you're not. He indulged in every known vice and you ...

Nigel What about me?

Mary Never mind.

Nigel Mary, I have drunk from it.

Mary That's disgusting.

Nigel Why? It's just an everyday skull.

Mary I'm going to get you some supper before I go out. All you've got swilling around inside you are those pills and a gallon of red wine ... (*She moves to the door*)

Nigel Mary — that dog came back. It was scratching at the door. When I opened it — it was gone ...

Mary (*studying Nigel*) I'll make some black coffee as well.

She exits

Nigel looks around the room nervously

Nigel (*uneasily*) I think I'll come through for it ... (*He switches off the light and opens the hall door*)

There is a faint tinkling sound followed by a rush of air

Nigel turns

> *There is a blinding light and he sees standing before him the figure of Lord Byron in Regency costume. Byron fixes him with a cold, enigmatic smile*

Nigel falls back in horror

Black-out

SCENE 2

Nigel Burke's study. Evening. Two days later

The executive chair is facing the window

Mary enters with Turner Gould, Nigel's agent. He is in his mid-forties, with a trim haircut and a thin moustache and is dressed in neat, casual clothes. He throws his top coat down on a chair

Turner I'm sorry I couldn't come any sooner, Mary. How is he?

Mary It's not good, Turner.

Turner Can we talk?

Mary Yes. He's resting. (*She closes the door*) He's watching a video of Will Hay. He says it's the only way he can relax. Nothing else seems to work.

Turner (*staring*) He can only watch Will Hay.

Mary It's worse than that. He can only watch *Oh, Mr Porter*.

Turner It must be some sort of breakdown. He should take a holiday.

Mary How can he take a holiday? He can't even cross the road.

Turner Why not? It's quiet enough here. You're in the heart of the country.

Mary He thinks he's going to be run over by a cattle truck.

Turner (*sighing*) When he was in London it was a double-decker bus.

Mary And there's something else. He keeps gargling.

Turner Gargling?

Mary Ever since the other night — since he drank from this ... (*She indicates the goblet*)

Turner What is it?

Mary It's a goblet made from a human skull.

Turner My God! This is something else, Mary.

Mary I know. I'm worried about him. He's been deeply depressed ever since Brighton. He thinks Michael has gone off the play.

Turner He's right. Michael finally turned it down.

Mary Oh, no. We can't tell Nigel that.

Turner Why not? Perhaps we should tell him to pull himself together.

Mary I don't think that's a good idea, Turner.

Turner We could say it's a challenge. Remember his first play? The one Michael rejected? He rewrote that in forty-eight hours and it was a hit.

Mary That was a long time ago and he was sleeping in those days. He had six pillows under him last night, Turner.

Turner (*impressed*) Six?

Mary He was almost vertical. I could have hung him in the wardrobe. He just sat there staring. It was like going to bed with a night watchman.

Turner What was he watching?

Mary The door. I found a chair propped against it this morning.

Turner But why?

Mary Turner, something happened the other night.

Turner What?

Mary I don't know. He wouldn't tell me. He had some sort of seizure. It wasn't surprising — all that wine on an empty stomach.

Turner He's drinking too much.

Mary And there's something else. He wants to change his name to Erik Bungle.

Turner He wants to change his name to what?

Mary Erik Bungle.

Turner Why?

Mary He has this conspiracy theory. He thinks the critics hate him. That they resent his early success. So he wants to change his name to Erik Bungle.

Turner I'd better have a word with him.

Mary I'll tell him you're here. (*She crosses to the door*)

Turner Mary.

She turns

That is all that's worrying him?

Mary (*after a pause*) Yes — that's all.

She exits

Turner looks distastefully at the goblet and moves it away from him. He studies the work on Nigel's desk

Nigel enters holding Julia's script — now dog-eared — and humming cheerfully

Turner (*looking surprised*) Feeling better, Nigel?
Nigel Better?
Turner Mary said you couldn't sleep ...
Nigel I have been a little depressed, Turner, but I've just read something that's cheered me up enormously. (*He throws the script down on the coffee table*) I've just read a play of such stupendous banality, such crushing tedium, such monumental tastelessness, so clichéd, so wooden, so melodramatic as to be almost funny. Are you listening, Turner? The vicar hangs himself from his own bell rope and as the curtain falls we hear the reproachful ding-dong, ding-dong across the meadow as he swings to and fro in the belfry.
Turner Who wrote it?
Nigel Julia Phillips. She's coming to collect it tonight. I don't know how I'm going to keep a straight face. Although I should thank her — she's made me realize how good I really am ...

Turner is silent

(*Becoming concerned*) What's the matter? You've heard something.
Turner Michael's not going to do the play.
Nigel (*drily*) Well, thank you for letting me down gently, Turner. (*He pauses*) Was it Brighton?
Turner The reviews didn't help. But Michael found it tepid.
Nigel Tepid!
Turner He said it lacked passion. (*He pauses*) Or was it compassion? I'm not sure. Anyway, he feels it needs work.
Nigel (*beadily*) And what's your opinion, Turner?
Turner What?
Nigel How do you feel it went at Brighton?
Turner I thought it went well.
Nigel Then why did you fall asleep in the second act?
Turner I didn't.
Nigel You were seen.
Turner Who saw me?

Nigel The director saw you. I saw you. And eventually Michael saw you. I'm only surprised the cast didn't see you. My own agent couldn't stay awake — how do you think that looked?

Turner I was jet–lagged. I may have nodded off briefly ...

Nigel You didn't just nod off. I could have endured that. Your face was turned upwards — your mouth was open and your head was resting on the shoulder of the woman next to you. People thought you were dead, Turner. There was considerable relief when you joined in the applause at the end.

Turner I was tired. I had read the play.

Nigel And what were your first words to me afterwards? "Where do we eat?"

Turner I said I enjoyed the play.

Nigel Sometime after the pudding, Turner. What a night. I haven't been out since.

Turner Nigel, I still believe in that play. And we're going to get it on. Mark my words "The Lost Cause" will go into the West End.

Nigel (*frowning*) Turner, it's called "The Last Cause". (*He sighs*) No wonder I'm going neurotic.

Turner Yes. I was going to talk to you about that. Mary said something happened the other night — something frightened you. What was it?

Nigel (*hesitating*) I was going to tell you ...

Turner Yes?

Nigel It was just after I drank from this goblet ...

Turner Go on.

Nigel (*hesitating*) Do you believe in ghosts, Turner?

Turner Ghosts? I have an open mind.

Nigel I saw Lord Byron.

Silence

Turner Lord Byron?

Nigel Yes.

Turner The poet.

Nigel Yes.

Turner Here?

Nigel Yes.

Turner In this room?

Nigel Yes.

Turner You must have been as pissed as a fart.

Nigel Is that what you call an open mind?

Turner Well, of course you saw him. You're surrounded by his pictures. And you'd been drinking.

Nigel You think it was an hallucination?

Turner Yes. You should get out more. You're becoming morbid. Do you know what I'm going to do? I'm going to take you both to *The Plough* for dinner.

Nigel I haven't been out for months.
Turner Then I suggest you make the effort. You should be all right — the cattle trucks have stopped running.
Nigel I think Mary's preparing something.
Turner Then I'll stop her.

He exits

Nigel examines the goblet thoughtfully

Potter appears in the garden, looking in through the window

Nigel becomes aware of being watched and looks up to see Potter watching him. He crosses to the door and admits Potter

Nigel Yes, Mr Potter?
Potter I thought I'd wait until you were alone. I didn't want to discuss our business in front of a third party. I am, of course, referring to that certain item in your possession.
Nigel Mr Potter, would you stop talking like Sidney Greenstreet. You mean the skull goblet?
Potter Yes.
Nigel I don't want it.
Potter But I thought you had a passionate interest in the subject. If it's a question of price ——
Nigel No. I find its presence disturbing. You may have noticed that I am of a nervous disposition. See my hands? See how they're shaking? I'm extremely tense, Mr Potter.
Potter We're all extremely tense, Mr Burke. There's nothing unusual in that. It's the times we live in.
Nigel You don't look tense.
Potter Don't judge by appearances. I'm like a duck crossing a pond: on the surface — calm and unruffled; but underneath I'm paddling away like fury. Look at my hands, Mr Burke.

They compare their trembling hands

Nigel Yes ...
Potter Now, what made you change your mind?
Nigel I think I'm going mad.
Potter We're all going mad. Join the club. It's a condition of the human race. Some of us hide it better, that's all.
Nigel I'm told I have a persecution complex.
Potter That's probably because you're being persecuted.

Nigel Do you think so?

Potter I've read your reviews, Mr Burke. You're being persecuted. We're all being persecuted. Critics ... wives ... (*bitterly*) ... mothers.

Nigel It's not just that. (*He hesitates*) I saw something that wasn't there.

Potter Now you join the cream of the country, the Cabinet itself, the best of our politicians. They've seen something that isn't there, that no one else can see.

Nigel What's that?

Potter The green shoots of recovery. Have you seen them? I haven't. And no one else has. We all see things we want to see, Mr Burke. (*He studies Nigel*) Was it Byron?

Nigel How did you know?

Potter It was when you mentioned the dog. Animals are often used as familiars by the spirit world.

Nigel You don't believe that, surely?

Potter Mr Burke, I have knowledge of a cat in Towcester who could cure you of sciatica and piles — assuming you suffered from those conditions — simply by sitting on your lap. How do you account for that?

Nigel I can't. But how do you know it wasn't an hallucination?

Potter At Newstead we've all been aware of Byron's unquiet spirit. Sometimes a distant figure at the end of a gallery when the visitors have left, occasionally the sight of a man in a ruffed shirt wandering the grounds. His presence is everywhere. In fact we once tried to get in touch with him by means of a ouija board.

Nigel What happened?

Potter Well, it is a primitive form of communication. But when we asked if Byron was there — the answer that came back was unmistakable. Yep.

Nigel (*suppressing a smile*) Yep? Lord Byron said yep?

Potter (*frowning*) I did say it was a primitive form of communication. We got a letter wrong.

Nigel Did you ask him anything else?

Potter Yes. We asked him if he was troubled.

Nigel What did he say?

Potter There was no reply.

Nigel Not even ... yep?

Potter There was no reply because the board was turned over as if in a fury.

Nigel I'm sorry, Mr Potter — I can't take this seriously.

Potter (*after a pause*) Did you know that Arnold Fisher had a similar experience?

Nigel The stonemason? The man who took the goblet?

Potter Yes. Apparently the skull goblet had a profound effect on him. From being a shy, retiring man uncertain of his physical attraction his success with women became phenomenal. He became widely known in the Nottingham area for his passionate nature.

Nigel (*intrigued*) Passionate?

Potter Yes. He even developed a slight limp that women found strangely appealing. His brother thought it was to avoid conscription — there was a war on at the time. But Arnold denied this and showed a strong desire to serve — apparently he had a burning wish to liberate Greece.

Nigel (*smiling*) Now, Mr Potter, I'm a writer and that was one line too many. I admire your sales pitch but I'm not buying.

Potter You mean you prefer to believe you're mad?

Nigel Well, no ——

Potter Wouldn't you like to be sure?

Nigel How can I be sure?

Potter Keep the goblet. There's no hurry. My clients can wait ... (*He backs towards the door*)

Nigel But, Mr Potter ...

Potter And if you change your mind ... We'll discuss a price ...

Potter exits into the garden

Nigel picks up the goblet as if to follow and then changes his mind. He returns his attention to the goblet, taking a deep breath and filling it with wine. He drinks from the goblet and looks about the room apprehensively. He relaxes, picks up a script and sits down on the sofa to read

There is a creaking sound; Nigel becomes aware of it and turns to see that the executive chair is swinging gently back and forth. He approaches the chair

The chair swings abruptly round to reveal the lounging figure of Byron who is holding a script

Nigel Jesus Christ!

Byron (*smiling*) No — only Byron.

Nigel (*backing away*) What do you want? What are you doing here? Are you haunting me?

Byron rises and moves towards Nigel in a limping glide

Byron Why should I haunt you?

Nigel I've no idea.

Byron How do I know you're not haunting me?

Nigel Because you're dead.

Byron Am I?

Nigel Yes.

Byron I see. (*He pauses*) And you're not?

Nigel No. Do I look dead?

Byron (*studying Nigel*) It's hard to say on so brief an acquaintance. When did I die?

Nigel When you were thirty-six.

Byron That's no age.

Nigel Your father died at thirty-six.

Byron That's no reason why I should follow suit. Where did I die?

Nigel In Greece — at Missolonghi. Don't you remember?

Byron I remember feeling distinctly unwell and anything was preferable to Missolonghi — even death. But I didn't expect this. One moment I'm asleep awaiting the Day of Judgement — which with my history I wasn't looking forward to with any great relish — the next moment I find myself here with you. (*He limps across the room and turns*)

Nigel draws his gaze from the limp

So you think I'm a ghost?

Nigel There is an alternative but it's too dreadful to contemplate.

Byron What is that?

Nigel That you're a figment of my imagination which means I'm mad.

Byron A figment! I'm one of the greatest figures of the age. I'm not a figment of anyone's imagination. (*Scornfully*) Certainly not yours.

Nigel I said it was a dreadful alternative.

Byron I can think of a worse one.

Nigel What's that?

Byron That you're a figment of my imagination which means I'm mad. After all, there's a great deal of it in my family. My mother once bit through a dinner plate in her rage and her family tree included five murders, two hangings, one excommunication and a suicide.

Nigel Look — I can't be a figment of your imagination. You're dead.

Byron You will keep harping on that, won't you?

Nigel I know you're dead. I know where you're buried. Everyone does. They even dug you up to make sure.

Byron (*shocked*) Dug me up?

Nigel Yes. You were under the floor of St Mary's, Hucknall. One of three coffins piled on top of each other. Your foot was cut off and your heart and brains were in a jar; apart from that you looked reasonably good, but you were unmistakably dead.

Byron (*after a long pause*) Did you say ... Hucknall?

Nigel Yes, it's near Nottingham.

Byron (*sharply*) I know where Hucknall is. So it wasn't the Abbey.

Nigel You mean Newstead?

Byron I mean Westminster.

Nigel No, the Dean wouldn't have you. And your fellow peers didn't attend the funeral — they sent empty carriages.
Byron Empty carriages?
Nigel Yes.
Byron So, I was buried in a hole under a floor in Hucknall which is a hole in itself.
Nigel I'm afraid so.
Byron You know what this means? I buried my dog in a better place.
Nigel (*anxiously*) He's not with you, is he?
Byron (*regarding Nigel*) Why are you taunting me with this?
Nigel I didn't like the disparaging way you referred to my imagination. (*He pauses*) You've read my play, haven't you?
Byron Yes.
Nigel You don't like it.
Byron There's something wrong with the end, the middle's not too good — and I don't like the beginning. Apart from that, it lacks something.
Nigel Passion?
Byron Possibly. Perhaps I could help you. I've always felt that to write about life — one has to live it.
Nigel (*uneasily*) Well, yes ... up to a point ...
Byron When did you last have a woman?
Nigel (*shocked*) I'm married.
Byron I was including your wife.
Nigel Having a woman. We don't say that any more. It's a shared experience.
Byron Not for some. Your hero is unfaithful. Have you ever practised infidelity?
Nigel (*evasively*) Look, he's also a surgeon but I've never taken a leg off.
Byron Then you haven't.
Nigel (*apologetically*) I'm agoraphobic.
Byron What?
Nigel It's Greek — it means ——
Byron I know my Greek. You're afraid of the market place?
Nigel It means more than that. I'm afraid of most things.
Byron I begin to see why I'm here.
Nigel Why?
Byron I'm Byron. I liberate the repressed.

The door opens suddenly and Turner looks in

Turner Mary says you should come and get ready.
Nigel I won't be a moment.
Turner (*curiously*) I thought I heard you talking?
Nigel I was acting out a scene, Turner.

Turner Well, don't be long.

Turner exits

Nigel He didn't see you. You are a figment of my imagination.
Byron I'm not haunting him. Who is he?
Nigel Turner Gould. He's my agent.
Byron (*crossing and looking thoughtfully towards the hall*) How much do you pay him?
Nigel Ten per cent.
Byron He's robbing you.
Nigel How do you know?
Byron He's in there with your wife at the moment and he's taking more than ten per cent.
Nigel I don't believe you. That's a foul suggestion.
Byron (*smiling*) One moment: if I'm a figment of your imagination it was your suggestion ... (*During the following he backs towards the garden door, his eyes on the hall*)
Nigel (*slumping*) You're right. Everything else has gone wrong: why not that? It's all right for you, George. You woke up one morning to find yourself famous. I woke up to find myself forgotten. The trouble is, it's made me bitter. These days I can't hear of a neighbour's wall collapsing, or a friend's bankruptcy without a distinct lifting of the spirits ... (*He notices Byron moving away*) Where are you going?
Byron I'm leaving.
Nigel Why?
Byron They're coming in here ...
Nigel (*suspiciously*) But they can't see you.
Byron That's the trouble. I hate to be ignored.

He opens the garden door

Nigel Ah.
Byron What?
Nigel You're using the door.
Byron What do you suggest?
Nigel If you were a ghost you'd pass through the wall.
Byron I'd prefer to try that on my own first. I'd look rather silly if I bounced back into the room.
Nigel Not much of a ghost, are you?
Byron I'm not much of a figment either. If you can't get me through a wall you haven't much imagination. But then I know that — I've read your work ...

He exits into the garden with a slight bow

There is a rush of air into the room. Nigel moves to close the door and peers out into the garden

Turner and Mary enter and stare uneasily at Nigel

Nigel (*muttering*) Cheeky bastard. (*He turns and sees Turner and Mary*)
Mary Nigel, are you going to get ready? The table's booked for nine.
Nigel Right ... (*He gives them an odd little laugh*)

Nigel exits

Turner Did you hear that laugh, Mary? Chilling. And the way he was staring at nothing.
Mary He often does that.
Turner And does he often talk to himself?
Mary He does when he's working.
Turner But he's not working, Mary. And does he suddenly swear for no apparent reason?
Mary Often. He sometimes shouts "Bollocks" for no obvious reason at all.
Turner Why do you think he does that?
Mary He says it's because of some unbearable personal recollection.
Turner Mary, we all have unbearable personal recollections but we don't all shout "Bollocks". And what about this Byron business? What's your explanation for that?
Mary (*hesitating*) It is a full moon ...
Turner You're not suggesting he's influenced by the moon?
Mary His father was. It's a powerful force. If it can move tides I'm sure it can move Nigel. He was like this last month — until I got busy with the Mogadons. Did you know dogs won't sleep in the moonlight, Turner?
Turner No, I didn't, Mary.
Mary And if they do they cover their eyes with their paws.
Turner That's hardly scientific.
Mary Well, what's your explanation?
Turner Well, first of all, why Byron?
Mary I think it's the attraction of opposites. After all, Nigel's always been a little repressed.
Turner You don't have to tell me that. His play's supposed to be a romantic comedy and the couples don't even kiss. I'm not a psychiatrist but there are two forces at work here. There's the ego and the other thing.
Mary Other thing?
Turner The other thing. What's it called? Is it the id?

Mary The id? Yes, I think it is.

Turner Well, I think Nigel has repressed his ego — or possibly his id. One or the other. (*He pauses*) Or is it yin and yang?

Mary Yin and yang?

Turner It doesn't matter. The point is there's an inner conflict between his yin and yang — or his ego and the other thing and Byron represents this other ... super ego — that's it — super ego ... (*He stops*) Or is it doppelgänger?

Mary Doppelgänger? I don't understand any of this.

Turner The point I'm making is that Byron represents Nigel's desire to be free of the repression and indulge in experimental sex — bondage — sado-masochism — that sort of thing.

Mary I see. So you think if Byron has his way Nigel will begin to indulge in experimental sex — bondage — sado-masochism — that sort of thing?

Turner Yes.

Mary (*grinning mischievously*) I don't see how I can lose, Turner.

Turner (*frowning*) Mary, I wish you wouldn't talk like that.

Mary (*putting her arms around Turner*) Sorry, Turner — I didn't mean ...

Turner puts a finger to his lips, moves to the hall door and listens. He opens the door

Nigel is standing on the threshold. He enters

Mary (*quickly*) Nigel, you're not even ready and it's almost nine.

Nigel I've just remembered Julia Phillips.

Mary Julia Phillips?

Nigel She's calling for her script. I'd better give her a few more minutes. You go ahead — I'll join you ...

He shepherds Turner and Mary into the hall

Mary (*off*) You know you won't come ...

Nigel (*off*) I will. In the meantime you've got plenty to talk about — if it's only me. (*He gives another odd little laugh*)

There is the sound of the front door closing

Julia appears in the garden. During the following she stares curiously in through the open garden door to the study

Nigel enters the study and sits at his desk

Bollocks!

He looks up and sees Julia staring at him

Julia.
Julia I saw the light on in here. I didn't want to disturb anyone else. (*She comes into the room*)
Nigel That's all right. They've gone to *The Plough*. Drink?
Julia Just a small one.

He pours. She watches him anxiously

Well?
Nigel What?
Julia (*picking up her script*) Have you read it?
Nigel Oh. Yes.
Julia Don't say you found it interesting; I couldn't bear that.
Nigel No, of course I didn't.
Julia (*staring*) What?
Nigel You've made a bold beginning, Julia.
Julia Have I?
Nigel Yes ... very bold ... if a little naïve.
Julia Oh. I didn't think anyone could accuse me of being naïve.
Nigel It's just that you haven't found your voice yet. You don't mind me saying this?
Julia No. (*She studies the script*) It's very crumpled.
Nigel What is?
Julia The script.
Nigel I have read it several times.
Julia Is this butter?
Nigel Just well thumbed, Julia.
Julia And these rings. Are they wine stains? It was in a plastic cover.
Nigel Yes, it was beautifully laid out. You've obviously had secretarial training, Julia.
Julia (*frowning*) Well, yes ...
Nigel And it shows.
Julia What's wrong with it?
Nigel (*taking a deep drink from the goblet*) Well, lesbianism, incest, homosexuality, woman priests are important themes. But you can overdo things. Take the rape.
Julia Which one?
Nigel (*staring*) You mean there are two?
Julia I thought you'd read it.
Nigel I must have turned a couple of pages over. But that's my point, Julia. You've over-egged the pudding. As a housewife you'll understand what I mean.

Julia (*grimly*) A housewife?

Nigel And there's something else. Don't be afraid of irony. Laugh at yourself before others do it for you. And some of these incidents do bring a smile unbidden to the lips. Particularly when the old vicar swings from his own bell rope. My lips did begin to pucker a little.

Julia They were meant to.

Nigel Pardon?

Julia It was meant to be funny.

Nigel Well, I don't think the Royal Court will see it that way.

Julia But they do. They're going to do it in the spring.

Nigel What! Why didn't you tell me?

Julia I just wanted to hear what you'd say. I knew you wouldn't like it. It's not your sort of thing, is it?

Nigel Oh. And what is my sort of thing?

Julia Well-crafted ... slightly predictable ... soufflés.

Nigel Soufflés!

Julia And as a housewife I can appreciate them. They're very enjoyable but they could have been written any time in the last thirty years.

Nigel What!

Julia All the characters speak with your voice, even the women out there in the kitchen, submitting to casual embraces and all that male arrogance. It's as if the sexual revolution had never taken place. It's hardly fearless or significant drama.

Nigel Ah, now I see where I'm going wrong. My next play is going to be about a psychopath with Aids who date rapes a one-legged, anorexic housewife who's married to an out-of-work child molester. I'm sure you'd like that one.

Julia Really, Nigel, I ——

Nigel I may not be fearless or significant but old ladies write to me thanking me for improving the quality of their lives. They watch my plays and enjoy them without offence because I have standards. I may not be significant but laughter is a healing influence — and if I don't cure the ills of this world I certainly help to bind the wounds. (*He drinks from the goblet*)

Julia I thought you'd take my criticism better than this, Nigel.

Nigel Well, life's full of disappointments. (*He pauses*) Who's directing?

Julia David Blake.

Nigel David. That explains it.

Julia Explains what?

Nigel He's always had a weakness for women writers.

Julia You mean because he encourages them to compete in what is still a male preserve?

Nigel No, because he fancies them.

Julia Are you suggesting he's doing my play because he fancies me?

Nigel Julia, you're very attractive. I know that must come as a terrible blow to you but you are physically advantaged. And once David had noticed the lipstick and the perfume, and realized that you weren't ... differently pleasured, I'm sure he couldn't wait to work with you.

Julia (*angrily*) That's typical of your attitude — trying to put my success down to my looks.

Nigel If you'd been some old crone you'd have been straight out the door. And don't worry about male prejudice — it's usually directed against men. And if you don't think looks matter why do you toss your hair, and pout, and laugh that fluted laugh?

Julia You really are despicable, aren't you? (*She turns away*)

Nigel I hope you're not going to cry, Julia. That would be so feminine, and so predictable. But that's the trouble with women: so predictable.

She turns and throws her drink over him. He looks surprised

Julia Well, you didn't predict that, did you?

Nigel takes Julia by the shoulders as if to shake her and then suddenly kisses her

Nigel And you didn't predict that.

She stares at him for a moment and then returns the kiss fiercely. They fall into a passionate embrace

Potter appears at the window and presses his face against the glass

CURTAIN

ACT II

SCENE 1

Nigel's study. Evening. Two weeks later

Nigel is working at his desk. A subtle change has come over him; his appearance is rakish, almost Byronic. There is mud on his shoes

There is the sound of Mary's footsteps approaching. Nigel registers this and bends more intently over his papers

Mary enters. She regards Nigel thoughtfully

Mary That woman rang again.

Nigel What woman?

Mary Julia Phillips.

Nigel (*pondering*) Julia ... ?

Mary Phillips. Surely you haven't forgotten already? The woman you hate. The woman who called the other week.

Nigel Oh, *that* Julia Phillips — forgotten her name for the moment.

Mary Funny — you've never had any trouble remembering her name before. It's usually "God, not another interview with Julia Phillips — what's she maundering on about this time." "A day in the life of Julia Phillips." "Julia Phillips' favourite walk." "Inside Julia Phillips' handbag." "Julia Phillips' most unforgettable shag." Now do you remember?

Nigel Of course. Do you know what I think? That I'm subconsciously trying to put her out of my mind.

Mary Is that why you won't return her calls?

Nigel I'm too busy.

Mary She seems determined. (*She pauses*) What happened that night?

Nigel What night?

Mary The night she came here. The night you didn't come to the restaurant.

Nigel We talked about her play.

Mary Nigel, have you fallen out of love with me?

Nigel Don't be silly, Mary.

Mary That's not an answer. I know you have a phobia about the word love, Nigel, but speak plainly.

Nigel No — I haven't fallen out of love with you.

Mary Then you're not having an affair?

Nigel No.

Mary And you're not chasing after anyone?

Nigel Mary, I'm agoraphobic. How can I chase after anyone? They only have to get beyond the door and they're safe.

Mary I had thought about that. So it would have to be someone who called. Now the cleaning lady's over seventy. That leaves the vicar's wife ...

Nigel (*shocked*) The vicar's wife!

Mary She is calling quite regularly.

Nigel She wants me to address the W.I. ...

Mary Then there's the Avon lady. I seem to be acquiring a great deal of make-up lately.

Nigel Her husband's written a play.

Mary Then there's the visiting chiropodist.

Nigel She's more interested in my bunion.

Mary Still, she finds you attractive — most women do.

Nigel (*grinning*) Do they? I didn't know.

Mary Didn't you? Then why are you grinning? And then of course there's Julia Phillips.

Nigel But I hate Julia Phillips.

Mary Hate's a strong emotion, Nigel. I'd prefer it if you found her boring.

Nigel I hate her because she's boring. Don't you trust me?

Mary (*studying him*) How do I know? How do I know what you're really like when I'm not with you? How do you think about me? How you talk about me?

Nigel That's something you have to take on trust, Mary. Like the light going out when you close the fridge door.

Mary And does your light go out when I close the door, Nigel?

Nigel Yes. How can you doubt it? Remember last night? Wasn't that a romantic evening ... ? The candlelight ... the wine ... ?

Mary It would have been nicer if we could have gone out.

Nigel (*moving closer*) But surely it meant something ...

Mary Nigel, even when the *Titanic* was sinking the band played on.

Nigel We're not sinking, Mary.

Mary Aren't we?

Nigel (*wheedling*) Mary, you're forgetting what happened afterwards.

Mary How could I? That's about as regular as our anniversary.

Nigel It was nothing like our anniversary.

Mary No. (*She moves to the door*) It was more like Pancake Day. You think "This is nice. Why don't we have it more often?" Then we don't have it again until Shrove Tuesday.

Nigel Mary, if I did have an affair ... What would you do?

Mary I'd kill you.

Nigel (*alarmed*) Kill me. But when your brother had an affair with his secretary you were very understanding. You said he'd fallen out of love with Angela and that's all there was to it.

Mary Nigel, other people's love affairs are like other people's heart attacks — we don't take them as seriously as our own. And I haven't looked after you all these years to lose you to someone else.

Nigel You'd lose me if you killed me.

Mary Death's one thing, Nigel — infidelity's another.

Nigel But supposing you'd been unfaithful to me, Mary ... would that make a difference?

Mary (*sharply*) Are you suggesting I've been unfaithful?

Nigel (*startled*) No.

Mary (*advancing*) Do you have proof?

Nigel No.

Mary Do you suspect me of being unfaithful?

Nigel No.

Mary And if I were unfaithful whose fault would it be?

Nigel Mine. But I don't suspect you. I trust you, Mary.

She regards him for a moment

Mary You don't trust me, Nigel. You just don't care. (*She crosses to the hall door and turns*) And if you're agoraphobic ... how did you get mud on your shoes?

She exits

Nigel Damn. (*He tries to rub the mud from his shoes*)

The garden door rattles as if someone has walked into it

Nigel allows himself a slight smile

The door opens and Byron enters looking peeved

Nigel She suspects, George. She thinks the only difference between our marriage and the *Titanic* was that they had a band.

Byron What was the *Titanic*?

Nigel A ship that was considered to be impregnable — it had its bottom ripped out by an iceberg and sank.

Byron smiles

Why do you smile?

Byron That description is faintly reminiscent of Lady Byron.

Nigel It's not funny, George. I blame you for this; it was all your idea.

Byron Nigel, if I'm a figment of your imagination it was all your idea.

Nigel Don't start that again.

Byron What happened?

Nigel She asked me if I'd fallen out of love with her. I said I hadn't.

Byron So you lied to her. Nothing unusual in that. Men have always lied to women — and women have always lied to themselves. It's the way of the world.

Nigel Actually, it wasn't a lie.

Byron You mean you still love her?

Nigel I mean I never loved her in the first place.

Byron What?

Nigel I loved someone else.

Byron And she refused you?

Nigel No, I didn't ask her. I didn't think she'd have me. Funny; I've never told anyone that before.

Byron Nigel, what a mistake. You asked nothing from love when you should have asked everything. Then why Mary?

Nigel We lived near each other. She wanted to get married ...

Byron Now I see. Your tragedy is that you didn't marry your dream — Mary's tragedy is that she did.

Nigel You're full of wise words, aren't you?

Byron I'm not blaming you. You alighted on the nearest perch; that was always a weakness of mine.

Nigel Yes, but you've alighted on a few more perches than I have, George.

Byron I couldn't resist the adventure.

Nigel Adventure! You married for money.

Byron That was a mistake.

Nigel It was for her. Remember what you said when Annabella Millbank consented to marry you? "It never rains but it pours." You were insulting to her in the coach coming from the wedding. You had her on the sofa before dinner. And in the middle of the night you woke up and cried, "God, I'm in hell."

Byron I was in an impossible situation

Nigel What impossible situation?

Byron Marriage. The truth is I've never thought women should live with us, Nigel. I'm not even sure they should eat with us.

Nigel And you're giving me all this advice. The truth is your life was a mess and now you've got me doing the same thing. I made a pass at the vicar's wife yesterday. I couldn't believe it.

Byron It was a more than a pass, Nigel. You pulled her down in the long grass — in the churchyard.

Nigel I know. I don't know what came over me. One moment we were talking about the Women's Institute, the next moment we were wrestling in the grass, in November, on a grave! And she was wearing her best tweed suit and a brave little hat. And if I hadn't stopped ...

Byron Why did you stop?

Nigel I looked up at the gravestone and it seemed to blur ... Then I could see the letters "In memory of Nigel Burke. He stands by the throne."

Byron He stands by the throne? Isn't that a shade optimistic ... considering what you were doing?

Nigel I know. But I did stop myself. I said I thought we were being watched. And then she said something rather strange ... she said, "Do you mean by the little man?" I looked around but I couldn't see anyone.

Byron And was she very shocked?

Nigel No, that's just it. She wanted to meet me after Evensong! It's you. I was never like this. It's like opening my eyes under water for the first time. I thought it would sting but it doesn't, and now I see a different world, full of the most incredible shapes ...

Byron Like the vicar's wife?

Nigel Yes. (*He pauses*) And the lady chiropodist ...

Byron What?

Nigel She was doing my foot today, George. Mary was out. She handled it so delicately, almost as if it were a bird ... about to fly away.

Byron Yes ... ?

Nigel I said I supposed she saw a lot of feet ... and she said she did ... and I asked her how mine compared ...

Byron And?

Nigel She said mine were rather sweet although for a man who never went anywhere they were rather careworn. I said I did a lot of pacing. I could hear her breathing. And then suddenly before I realized what I was doing I placed my bare foot against her white coat — on her breast.

Byron And what did she do?

Nigel She kissed my toes.

Byron And then?

Nigel And then the Avon lady called.

Byron The Avon lady?

Nigel She sells paints and powders. (*He frowns*) Unfortunately she doesn't seem to have any kiss-proof lipstick. And she talks. Suppose she compares notes with the vicar's wife? Suppose the vicar finds out? We could have him swinging from his own bell rope.

Byron (*smiling*) Well, at least I've opened your eyes, Nigel.

Nigel George, I can't go round the village like a Regency buck.

Byron You're not going round the village — you're doing it from home.

The door opens and Turner enters carrying a playscript

Nigel Turner. I didn't know you were here.

Turner puts the playscript gingerly down on Nigel's desk

Nigel Well?
Turner (*slowly*) I love that play, Nigel.
Nigel (*suspiciously*) Yes?
Turner And I'd still say that if you put me on the rack but ...
Nigel But?
Turner The theatre's in a terrible state at the moment ...
Nigel It's always been in a terrible state — or do you think I'm going to make it worse?
Turner No.
Nigel You don't like it.
Turner You've altered it.
Nigel Of course I've altered it. That's why it's called a rewrite.
Turner But it's not your usual style.
Byron (*quietly*) Amen to that.
Nigel Shut up.
Turner Nigel.
Nigel How do you mean it's not my usual style?
Turner Well, for one thing, it's erotic. You've never been erotic before.
Nigel Then perhaps it's time I was.
Turner And there's something else. The husband walks out at the end.
Byron That was my idea.
Nigel (*sharply*) That was my idea.
Turner I know, but he stayed in the original. Michael liked that ending. It is light comedy, Nigel.
Byron It would have been a tragedy if he'd stayed.
Nigel It would have been a tragedy if he'd stayed ... (*He frowns at Byron*)
Turner Even so, I don't think we should show it to Michael — not yet. Perhaps we could try it out somewhere. You could use that name — Erik Bungle. I know of this tram shed in Islington ... just opened ...
Nigel Tram shed! You hate it.
Turner No. But it's not for Michael.
Nigel Turner — I've already sent it to Michael.
Turner (*staring*) What? I can't believe I'm hearing this. How long have we known each other, Nigel?
Nigel (*sighing*) A long time.
Turner (*solemnly*) A long time. And in all that time we've had no secrets ...
Nigel Haven't we?
Turner No. We've done everything together, Nigel.

Nigel Have we?

Turner Or am I just an agent?

Nigel No ... you're more than that.

Turner I'm a friend, Nigel. In some ways I feel I've taken the place of your late father.

Nigel He's still alive, Turner.

Turner (*surprised*) Oh, is he? Still, he hasn't been much use to you since he saw those little yellow men, has he?

Nigel They were green.

Turner When you came to London touting your dog-eared scripts up and down Shaftesbury Avenue, no one wanted to know. Your work was crude, clumsy and naïve. You couldn't even spell "champagne". And who liked your work? Who saw your talent?

Nigel You did, Turner.

Turner And who bought you lunch?

Nigel I've always appreciated that ——

Turner (*holding up his hand*) I don't want to hear about how many lunches I bought you when you couldn't afford to eat. But tell me, in all that time, has there ever been a contract, a written agreement — even a piece of paper between us?

Nigel No.

Turner Just a simple handshake all those years ago. And now you tell me that you sent the script to Michael without consulting me. I don't believe it. I can't believe I'm hearing this. As if I'm not always available. As if you couldn't have rung me.

Nigel Like this afternoon?

Turner Yes.

Nigel I did ring you.

Turner (*staring*) But you never use the phone.

Nigel I had to; Mary was out all day. You weren't there.

Turner I must have been in a meeting.

Nigel They said you'd taken the day off.

Turner I never take the day off.

Mary puts her head around the door

Mary Turner — your office is on the phone. They've been trying to get you all day.

Turner (*blustering*) I'm dealing with incompetents.

He exits

Mary gives Nigel an awkward smile and follows

Byron What did I tell you?
Nigel I don't want to hear about it.
Byron They were meeting.
Nigel Shut up!

The garden door opens abruptly and Julia makes an emotional entrance. She carries a bag

Julia!
Julia Why didn't you return my calls, Nigel?
Nigel I'm sorry, Julia. I didn't know what to say to you. (*To Byron*) Would you please go?
Julia I'm not leaving, Nigel.
Nigel I didn't mean ...
Julia We can't just forget what happened.
Nigel No, of course not.
Julia Didn't it mean anything or was it meant to be the final humiliation?
Nigel I didn't mean to humiliate you and I bitterly regret it.
Julia (*staring*) Regret it?
Nigel I mean for your sake. I can hardly believe it happened.

He darts an anxious glance towards the hall door

Julia You mean it made so little impression?
Nigel No.
Julia Then why, Nigel?
Nigel You're a beautiful woman, Julia.
Julia (*impatiently*) Don't say that.
Nigel But you are beautiful.
Julia I meant woman. Woman means victim. I'm a person, Nigel. A person in my own right.
Nigel Then you're a beautiful person.
Julia And you think that explains it? That's like the meat eater blaming the chicken for being tasty. You said you loved me. I'm surprised you've forgotten. You said it before, during and after.
Nigel And I meant it. I've loved you ever since I saw your picture on the book jacket of your first novel.

Byron smiles cynically

(*Catching sight of this*) Don't look like that.
Julia I can't help looking surprised, Nigel. Then why wouldn't you take my calls? Why wouldn't you see me?

Nigel There's Mary to consider; she may come in at any moment. You must go.

Julia Then come to me. I've taken a room at *The Plough*.

Nigel What!

Julia Come and see me — if it's only for a few minutes.

Nigel I can't — I'm agoraphobic.

Julia I know. Mary's made a point of telling me that on several occasions. Then wear these. (*She takes a soft hat, scarf and a pair of heavy glasses from the pocket of her coat*)

Nigel What are these for?

Julia My uncle was an agoraphobic. He overcame it by wearing a broad brimmed hat, heavy glasses and a muffler.

Nigel (*examining the items doubtfully*) I don't know, Julia ...

Julia Nigel, I have a particular reason for asking. Tonight's special ... (*She takes a newspaper from her bag*) Have you seen the *Guardian*? It's my birthday.

Nigel (*staring at the paper; shocked*) Your birthday's in the *Guardian*?

Julia Yes. See — Julia Phillips — novelist. Don't look at my age.

Nigel They print your birthday?

Julia Yes. Don't they print yours?

Nigel No. I've looked but it's always the Prime Minister and two biochemists. How did they know it was your birthday?

Julia I suppose they got it from *Who's Who*.

Nigel (*doubly shocked*) You're in *Who's Who*?

Julia Yes — aren't you?

Nigel No.

Julia That shows how silly it all is.

Nigel Yes ...

Julia It's not important. The important thing is that you come. I must see you. It's important. My writing's suffering.

Nigel (*hopefully*) Is it?

Julia I can't stop thinking about you. (*She kisses him*) I had to do that. I had to take the initiative. I must be in control. I don't want a master-slave relationship.

Nigel (*breathlessly*) Nor do I.

Julia I won't be submissive.

Nigel I don't want you to be.

Julia There'll be times when I shall be dominant ...

Nigel I'd like that ...

They hold each other for a moment

But you must go ...

He guides her to the garden door, walking with a slight limp

Julia Nigel, you're limping.
Nigel Yes ... I must see my chiropodist ...

They embrace at the door

Julia You will come?
Nigel I'll try.
Julia God. I love you.

Julia gives Nigel one more despairing kiss and exits

Nigel turns and sees Byron regarding him coldly

Nigel I thought I told you to go?
Byron Why are you limping, Nigel? Are you mocking me?
Nigel No. (*Nastily*) I just find that it arouses a woman's sympathy.
Byron (*angrily*) You think I did it for that? I fought, I loved, I swam the
Hellespont. I excelled in all things. And do you know why? Because once
upon a time I heard a young girl say, "I couldn't marry that poor lame boy".
The limp made Byron but you can't be Byron just by limping ...

There is a rush of air and the Lights fade to Black-out

Byron exits

The Lights come up again

Turner enters the room excitedly

Nigel turns to him

Turner It was Michael. He asked me to ring him at home. Are you ready for
this, Nigel? He loves the play.
Nigel I thought he would.
Turner He saw what I saw. He saw the strength, he saw the passion — or
was it compassion? I'm having lunch with him tomorrow. We're going to
be rich, Nigel.
Nigel (*coldly*) We're going to be rich? Then you intend to ask for your
commission?
Turner What?
Nigel I sent the play to Michael. You wanted to do it in a tram shed.
Turner Nigel, we're not going to quibble about who actually posted the play,
are we? I recognized its quality.

Nigel Turner, you wouldn't recognize a good play if it got up in front of you and danced a jig. Now, ring Michael and arrange lunch for three.

Turner Three?

Nigel Unless you don't want to come.

Turner Nigel, I don't want to put obstacles in your path but how can you keep a lunch appointment when you can't get to the bottom of the garden? And don't forget your morbid fear.

Nigel What morbid fear?

Turner Of choking to death in a public place. You know how your throat constricts in restaurants.

Nigel Turner, I'm not sitting here like a bloody battery hen whilst you do all the talking. Ring Michael or I will.

Turner Yes, Nigel.

Turner exits

Nigel hesitates and then reaches for the hat and scarf

Mary enters

Mary Turner's just told me. Isn't it wonderful? I'm opening some champagne. Are you coming through?

Nigel Not just yet ...

Mary Oh, by the way. There was a message on the answering machine. *Who's Who* want to know your personal details.

Nigel (*shocked*) *Who's Who*?

Mary They want to know your hobbies.

Nigel I haven't got any.

Mary We'll say long walks and scuba diving. Well, you have to say something.

Nigel *Who's Who*. (*He picks up the goblet reverently and drinks from it*) So, it's happened at last. The Prime Minister, two bio-chemists ... and me.

Mary (*picking up the hat and scarf*) I haven't seen these before.

Nigel Haven't you? (*He takes the hat from her and puts it on*)

Mary What are you doing?

Nigel I'm going for a walk.

Mary But that's wonderful.

Nigel Yes.

Mary I'll come with you.

Nigel No. I have to do this alone.

Mary Are you sure? Perhaps you'd better take a Valium.

Nigel No.

Mary Where are you going?

Nigel Why?

Mary Well, suppose something happens? I heard a heavy truck go by a while ago — and it's a narrow lane — and it's dark.

Nigel Do I have to account for my every move, Mary?

Mary No, of course not. I'll leave supper — probably go for a jog ... (*She pauses*) You won't be long?

Nigel (*shrugging*) That depends.

Mary stares at Nigel for a moment and then exits

Nigel slips on the hat and scarf. He opens the garden door

Potter is standing on the threshold

Nigel Mr Potter. I'd almost forgotten you. I suppose you've come about the goblet.

Potter Well, yes, Mr Burke. (*He comes into the room*)

Nigel (*removing the hat and scarf and throwing them on a chair*) And you wonder what I consider a fair price.

Potter No, it's not that. The people I represent have changed their minds. They don't wish to sell.

Nigel Why not?

Potter They've been advised in the matter — and they would like the goblet to be returned.

Nigel Who advised them?

Potter I did.

Nigel But you wanted me to buy it. Mr Potter, I have no intention of returning the goblet. We've already established the family had no proper title. It was stolen. I intend to keep the skull goblet until I decide what to do with it. (*He pours more wine into the goblet*)

Potter It would be dangerous for you to keep it, Mr Burke.

Nigel Why?

Potter When I came before I had not been given the full story. Further enquiries have revealed some disturbing facts ...

Nigel What disturbing facts?

Potter You remember I told you of a significant change in Arnold Fisher once he obtained the skull goblet?

Nigel Yes: he became irresistible to women.

Potter That, unfortunately, was only part of the story. His brother William left an account of Arnold Fisher's last days and it doesn't make pleasant reading. I told you how Arnold had changed — of his great physical attraction. Even his work as a stonemason was transformed, attracting much interest and admiration, although some thought his cherubs exotic, even disturbing. He appeared at the peak of his physical and creative powers. Even so, he spent many hours alone in his room drinking. His brother, who had the room below, often heard him talking late into the night, low and intense, then a strange sound across the floorboards, a shuffling sound as if someone was limping about the room. Arnold Fisher's manner grew strange and fearful in those last days and he always kept his door locked. But on the night he died his brother heard a scream of fear. He burst into Arnold's room and found him drinking from the skull goblet. The red wine was spilt across his shirt like blood and he was as pale as a ghost. William asked what had frightened his brother: all Arnold could say was, "It was the other one."

Nigel The other one?

Potter That was all he said. William returned to his room and the shuffling ceased. Then he heard a faint sound, a sound he hadn't heard before. A sound not unpleasant but strangely sinister. He said it was like sacred music but not of today. Have you heard anything like that, Mr Burke?

Nigel No.

Potter Good. Because when they found Arnold Fisher the next morning he was dead and he'd died badly. His face was twisted in a grotesque mask of fear, his eyes were protruding, his tongue was lolling out the side of his mouth, his hands were ——

Nigel All right, Potter. You can spare me the hands. You think Byron did that to him?

Potter Not Byron: "the other one".

Nigel Who is the other one?

Potter Didn't Byron say anything?

Nigel (*drinking from the goblet*) If you think I've been having conversations with a man who died over a hundred and fifty years ago ... (*He limps back from the desk*)

Potter Mr Burke, you're limping.

Nigel Am I?

Potter You can tell me, Mr Burke. You see, I believe. Did he mention the other one?

Nigel (*hesitating*) No.

Potter Perhaps he was too afraid.

Nigel Not Byron.

Potter Did you know that Byron never travelled without a loaded pistol, that he suffered from the night terrors and went cold with fright, that he was known to fall into a dead faint for no apparent reason?

Nigel Well, yes, but ——

Potter Did you know that a number of Byron's friends died young — the ones who came to Newstead and joined in the debauchery there?

Nigel Well, they did lead dissipated lives in those days.

Potter Or perhaps they saw "the other one".
Nigel But who is he? (*He drinks deeply from the goblet*)

Potter watches him

Potter Byron was very profane in his youth and there was always this
   fascination with skulls ...
Nigel Skulls?
Potter The skull goblet for example. The skull of a monk dug up in the Abbey
   grounds and made into a goblet by Byron.
Nigel What are you getting at, Mr Potter?
Potter The sacred music, not of today — possibly a Gregorian chant? And
   there was something else William Fisher saw that night. When he looked
   from the window he thought he saw the shadowy figure of a monk ...
Nigel A monk?
Potter I know who "the other one" is, Mr Burke. He's here now. You're
   holding him in your hand. You're drinking from him.
Nigel (*choking and putting the goblet down violently*) My God!
Potter Think of it. A simple monk who spent all his life in good works,
   resting in peace in the Abbey grounds and then dug up and forced to witness
   nightly scenes of drunken depravity. How would he feel? He'd feel that all
   the punishments of hell wouldn't atone for his suffering.
Nigel You think he may come back for his head?
Potter Or for you, Mr Burke. I have a dreadful premonition. Is it possible
   that the haunter has become the haunted and that Byron intends to put his
   ghost on to you?
Nigel (*alarmed*) No!
Potter This is the time when we're all most vulnerable, Mr Burke. The time
   of the year when the ancients commemorated the dead and the coming of
   winter. When they prayed for the return of the sun. When the veil between
   this world and the next is so transparent that we can almost see beyond ...
   That's how Byron reached you — and that's how "the other one" has
   reached him.
Nigel What am I going to do?
Potter (*taking a Harrods bag from the pocket of his raincoat*) Give me the
   goblet. I'll take it back to Newstead and bury it in the grounds. Pray God
   I'm not too late.

Nigel drops the goblet into the bag

Potter (*moving to the garden door*) And take care, Mr Burke.
Nigel And you, Mr Potter.

Potter pauses and listens

Potter What was that?
Nigel What?
Potter I thought I heard ... (*He pauses*) No ... perhaps not ...

Potter exits

Nigel draws the curtains and bolts the door. He glares at the bust of Byron

Nigel Where are you now, George? I notice you've made yourself scarce. Probably won't stop running until you get to Hucknall. (*He moves the hat and scarf to sit down, then stops*) My God! Julia. (*He hesitates, then listens at the door for a moment, then returns and slips on the hat and scarf. He hesitates and then adds the glasses. He unbolts the door*)

There is the faint sound of Gregorian chant. Nigel hears this and listens harder. The sound dies away. Nigel dismisses the sound, switches off the light and opens the garden door. The chant begins again. Nigel switches on the garden light and peers out. The chant grows louder and louder. Nigel falls back, whimpering

Suddenly a shadowy, hooded figure appears framed against the open door

Holy shit!

Nigel turns and dashes into the hall

The hooded figure enters and switches on the light. The chant stops. The figure is Mary in her track suit. She pulls down the hood and smiles

Turner enters from the hall

Turner Nigel's hiding under the stairs again. And I thought he was so much better. What happened?
Mary (*smiling*) I think I must have frightened him. (*She calls through the hall door*) Nigel, you can come out. There's no need to be afraid. There's no one here but us ...

Turner and Mary smile pleasantly at each other. Turner pours himself a drink

Turner His eyes were rolling.
Mary Poor Nigel.
Turner Now that's what I call a relapse.
Mary I knew he was rushing things.

Nigel enters cautiously

Are you all right, Nigel?

Nigel I thought I saw something ... (*He looks fearfully at the door*)

Mary Did you, darling? Never mind. That's your writer's imagination. You've always been too highly strung.

Nigel Highly strung. You could play me like a violin, Mary.

Mary Then I'm going to get you some tablets. (*She moves to the door and turns*) Will you be going out now?

Nigel Not tonight. I don't feel well.

Mary I'll get the tablets.

Nigel The big ones, Mary.

Mary Yes, darling. (*She pauses*) You look terrible.

Mary exits

Nigel begins searching the drawer of his desk

Nigel Oh, Turner ...

Turner Yes. Nigel?

Nigel You'd better ring Michael and arrange lunch for two. I don't really feel up to it ...

Turner (*smiling*) Right, Nigel.

Turner exits

Nigel takes the Chinese balls from the drawer. He looks around nervously and begins to juggle the balls furiously in his hands

CURTAIN

SCENE 2

Nigel's study. Early morning. Three months later

A table lamp illuminates the room. The executive chair is again facing the window

Julia is moving about the room putting on her coat. She glances impatiently at her watch

Nigel enters

Julia Where are your cases?

Nigel In the hall. (*He hesitates*) I've been thinking, Julia. Is this the time?

Julia Of course it's the time. It's the only time. It's the first time we've been together in three months and then only because you couldn't go to your first night.

Nigel Yes. (*He frowns*) I thought Mary would have rung by now.

Julia Well, when she does ring we won't be here.

Nigel I think I should wait for the call. It is important to me.

Julia Not as important as this. Now, forget the play for a moment and write the note.

Nigel Write the note?

Julia Explaining things to Mary.

Nigel Can't I just disappear?

Julia No.

Nigel Why not?

Julia Because she'll be dragging the river for you. (*She sets out pen and paper on the desk*)

Nigel What should I say?

Julia Tell her we've become lovers.

Nigel Lovers. I don't think she's ready for that. Can't we say friends? Close friends? Leave her to assume lovers?

Julia No. You do love me, don't you?

Nigel That goes without saying, Julia.

Julia It never goes without saying, Nigel. Just write the note. I can't stand this deceit any longer. If you'd told Mary in the first place ——

Nigel That we've become lovers? You couldn't say something like that to Mary and get away with it. "Oh, by the way, Julia and I have become lovers." You couldn't throw a remark like that into the conversation. It would be like throwing a leg of lamb into a pool of piranha — it would be chased up and down and devoured.

Julia Then write the note.

Nigel I don't know what to say.

Julia There is an alternative.

Nigel What?

Julia I could stay here and have it out with her.

Nigel (*alarmed*) Have it out with her!

Julia When she comes back in the morning.

Nigel Have it out with Mary? I can't have people coming here and having it out with people. My nerves won't stand it. I'm a sick man. This is my sanctuary. If you start having things out what happens to me?

Julia (*sighing*) Nigel, you're coming to live with me — remember?

Nigel Yes, well, I'm not sure about Holland Park, Julia. There are the lifts for one thing — I always feel trapped in lifts — and the stairs bring on my vertigo.

Julia It's a ground floor apartment.

Nigel Is it? Still, I suppose there'll be muggers in the hall, beggars with bedrolls and Rottweilers peeing in the stairwell.

Julia No pets. And it's quite select. Now write the note.

Nigel This isn't easy.

Julia If you're short of something to say, mention her affair with Turner Gould.

Nigel I'm not sure about that, Julia. It was just something Byron said.

Julia Please Nigel. I don't want to hear any more about Byron. We agreed it was an hallucination. You haven't seem him again?

Nigel No.

Julia You see how good I am for you.

Nigel Now it's the headless monk.

Julia Headless monk?

Nigel I know it's an hallucination but I thought I saw him tonight.

Julia (*after a pause*) In the bedroom?

Nigel Yes. (*He frowns*) Why?

Julia (*quickly*) Nothing.

Nigel (*regarding her suspiciously*) You sensed something.

Julia (*hesitating*) Yes.

Nigel What was it?

Julia Well, when I woke there was this ... damp smell.

Nigel Damp smell?

Julia As if a cellar had been opened for the first time in centuries ... And there was a slithering sound ...

Nigel Slithering. And was there ... chanting?

Julia Yes — chanting. And then I heard this rasping breath. First it seemed to come from the fireplace — then under the bed — and then everywhere. Did you hear it?

Nigel No, I was under the sheets.

Julia Then I saw a shape. A hooded figure at the end of the bed, with long
bony fingers ... working like pincers ...

Nigel Julia! Don't do that. You're scaring me shitless.

Julia (*breaking into a smile*) It's for your own good. (*She laughs*) I didn't
really see anything.

Nigel What?

Julia It's what they call flooding.

Nigel Flooding?

Julia You confront the patient with his worst fears until he becomes immune
to them. Flooding.

Nigel Julia, you try that again and I'll be the one who's flooding.

Julia It won't be so bad the next time. Mary's always pandered to your fears
and drugged you to the eyeballs. Now you have the chance to be your own
person at last. No one to tell you what to think. No one to tell you what to
do ... (*She crosses to the garden door and turns; briskly*) Now finish that
note and get your cases. I'll fetch the car — it's parked in the square.

Julia exits into the garden

Nigel frowns and returns to his note

There is a squeal of brakes outside

Nigel looks up in alarm and peers through the window

Nigel Oh, my God!

*He exits into the hall, and enters with two suitcases which he hides behind
the settee*

Mary enters, taking off her coat

Mary Did you hear those brakes? Turner thought he saw a dog.

Nigel A dog. What sort of dog?

Mary I said it was more likely a fox at this time of night but Turner said it
was too big.

Nigel How big was it? (*He stares out of the window*)

Mary Does it matter? Don't you want to hear about the play?

Nigel I don't need to — it was a disaster.

Mary No. It was a triumph.

Nigel I don't believe it. I thought once I'd got rid of the ... (*He hesitates*)

Mary (*regarding him curiously*) What?

Nigel (*lamely*) The goblet.

Mary Nigel, you're so superstitious. This has nothing to do with the goblet.
Carrington was there.

Nigel Carrington?

Mary I sat near him. And when the lights came up — he smiled.

Nigel (*doubtfully*) Carrington smiled?

Mary And I heard him say to his friend ——

Nigel (*surprised*) Carrington has a friend?

Mary — he said to his friend: "That was a treat."

Nigel considers this

Nigel You're sure it wasn't "Where do we eat?"

Mary No. Don't you believe me?

Nigel It's just that I have this premonition that something's going to go wrong. Where's Turner?

Mary He's ringing some people he knows on the night desks. He thinks the reviews are going to be excellent.

Nigel And did they like the new ending?

Mary (*slowly*) They appear to ... Although I have to say that was the one part of the play I didn't like ...

Nigel Why?

Mary I thought it was weak.

Nigel Weak?

Mary Well, it was unbelievable. He wouldn't have left his wife.

Nigel Why not!

Mary Because he'd never made a decision in his life: and people don't change, Nigel.

Nigel Don't they?

Mary Well, not that sort of person. He was such a wimp.

Nigel A wimp?

Mary Yes. He was a prey to every fear. He was prone to every wind that blew. He was nervous and terrified. A man like that wouldn't leave. He couldn't even pack his own suitcase.

Nigel Couldn't he?

Mary No, he was hopeless. And as for him leaving to go abroad — he wouldn't have got to the bottom of the road. He couldn't even drive a car.

Nigel Well, I can't ... (*He breaks off*)

Mary He was so spineless. I'm surprised she put up with him.

Nigel Spineless.

Mary Yes, although I must say the character was very well drawn and very funny. I said to Turner you must have taken him from life.

Nigel What?

Mary You must have based him on someone. You couldn't invent a character like that. Who was it?

Nigel Who was it?

Mary Yes.

Nigel (*after a long pause*) He was a sort of composite character ...

Mary I thought I saw traces of your father. (*She sees Nigel's note and picks it up*) Oh, is this for me?

Nigel What?

Mary (*opening the note: stares*) It's from you. It says, "Dear Mary, whatever happens — remember I loved you."

Nigel Yes.

Mary What's going to happen, Nigel?

Nigel Anything could happen, Mary, in my state of health.

Mary It says *loved* you — *past* tense.

Nigel If I were dead it would be in the past tense. I have this premonition, Mary.

Mary You've always had premonitions; you've never left me a note before. You're not going to die, Nigel; you're in the prime of life.

Nigel Byron died when he was thirty-six.

Mary Byron buggered everyone in sight; that's why he died at thirty-six. You're hardly in that league. (*She puts the note down and studies Nigel*) Have you been seeing things again?

Nigel I don't know ... I thought I saw something ...

Mary The headless monk?

Nigel I thought I saw him in the shadows ... watching me.

Mary Nigel, if he's headless, how can he watch you?

Nigel I don't know.

Mary You obviously haven't thought this through. And you're hyperventilating.

Nigel (*alarmed*) Am I? I thought I was just breathing.

Mary No, you're hyperventilating. I can tell by the way your shirt's going up and down. You've been thinking about breathing again, haven't you?

Nigel Yes. Well, I try not to think about it but once I do it becomes such an effort.

Mary Well, I wouldn't advise you to stop, Nigel. (*She feels his pulse*)

Nigel Don't you ever think about breathing, Mary?

Mary Never. I knew I shouldn't have left you. Do you know what I'm going to do? I'm going to get those new tablets. They're supposed to be wonderful. If I can remember where I put them. After all, this is a special occasion; we should celebrate. (*She kisses him on the forehead*) Poor Nigel. You'd be lost without me, wouldn't you.

Nigel Yes, Mary.

Mary exits

Nigel slumps on to the settee looking defeated. Something catches his eye. He pulls aside a cushion to reveal a Harrods bag. He puts his hand in gingerly and withdraws the skull goblet

My God! How did you get here? You must have bloody legs. You're supposed to be buried at Newstead.

There is a rush of air, a tinkling and the Lights fade to Black-out

The Lights come up

The executive chair is swinging to and fro

Nigel turns to look at the chair

The chair swings round to reveal the lounging figure of Byron

Nigel So you're back? What have you come for this time?
Byron I've come to say goodbye, Nigel.
Nigel (*cautiously*) Goodbye? How do you know it's goodbye?
Byron I know.
Nigel You mean I'm going to die, don't you?
Byron We're all going to die, Nigel.
Nigel You're not, you're dead.
Byron You will keep reminding me of that. So, the play went well?
Nigel (*nodding*) Carrington smiled.
Byron Carrington?
Nigel A critic.
Byron (*scornfully*) Critics. Nigel, seek roses in December, ice in June and constancy in a woman before you trust the word of a critic. Still, the play went well — and the ending?
Nigel I believe so.
Byron Good. Ends are difficult, in art, as in life ...
Nigel You are talking about death.
Byron I'm talking about your departure. You are leaving?
Nigel You don't think I should?
Byron I left Lady Byron.
Nigel You mean she left you.
Byron She merely left the house: I left the country.
Nigel You think I'm making a mistake, don't you?
Byron Who knows? Perhaps Mary was your phobia after all. Perhaps you've never been sick, only unhappy. But are you sure you're changing your life or merely changing your jailer?
Nigel What would you do?
Byron Nigel, if we subtract from life vegetating, sleeping, eating, shaving, swilling, buttoning and unbuttoning, how much remains of downright existence? The summer of a dormouse. And that's what you remind me of: a dormouse. Life can't be measured in years, only in action. And there's been precious little of it around here.

Nigel You're preparing me for something.

Byron The trouble is you've become so afraid of death you've become afraid of life, Nigel.

Nigel Look who's talking? Who travelled with loaded pistols?

Byron At least I travelled.

Nigel (*moving closer*) But why the pistols? Was it because of him? The other one?

Byron (*staring*) The other one?

Nigel (*raising the goblet*) Remember this, George? It's something I've noticed about you, that whenever you've come into this room you've never spoken of it, or looked at it, or acknowledged its presence in any way. You've ignored it. Why? When you were at Missolonghi and in your delirium you spoke to your manservant for a whole day in desperate tones but he never understood a word you uttered. What were you saying, George?

Byron I don't remember.

Nigel Was it about the goblet? (*He pours wine into the goblet and offers it to Byron*) Why don't you join me? Why don't you drink from it, George?

Byron (*shrugging*) I'm a ghost. I'd probably dribble.

Nigel Now it suits you to be a ghost. Drink.

Byron (*drawing back*) Nigel, I'm at the bar. Would you have me imperil my immortal soul?

Nigel George, during your life you were accused of murder, bigamy, piracy, incest, sodomy, buggery and devil worship. I don't think drinking from a goblet's going to make much difference. Did you see him at Missolonghi? Is he coming for me with his long bony fingers? Is he death?

Byron (*moving away*) I heard a saying when I was in the East. Death is a camel that lies across every door. Whoever the other one is. Death, fear or the terror that comes by night — we all have to face him — and we have to face him alone ...

The Lights begin to fade

Nigel (*irritably*) I must say you've been a great help. Did you know that Charlotte Brontë based Mr Rochester on you? He was a pain in the arse as well.

The Lights brighten for a moment

Byron (*angrily*) Take care, Nigel. You're talking to a man who could snuff a candle out at twenty paces — and if I wasn't a ghost I'd call you out.

Nigel And if I wasn't an agoraphobic I'd come ...

The Lights fade to Black-out

No, George, don't go. I didn't mean ...

Byron exits

The Lights come up

There is the distant sound of a car horn

God! Julia. (*He picks up the cases*)

Turner enters

Turner The reviews were wonderful ... (*He looks at Nigel curiously*) Going somewhere, Nigel?
Nigel Yes. I'm leaving Mary.
Turner Oh. Then you'd better hurry. She's a jogger. She'll soon catch you up.
Nigel You're not going to tell her?
Turner No. (*He pauses*) You know how I feel about Mary?
Nigel Yes.
Turner You don't want to talk about it?
Nigel I'd rather not.
Turner It's just that whilst you're around I don't seem to stand much chance ... (*He moves to the hall door*) I'll keep her talking. (*He pauses*) Who is it?
Nigel Julia Phillips.
Turner The writer?
Nigel Yes.
Turner Does she have an agent?
Nigel I don't know.
Turner Well, let me know where you are. I'll need to get in touch. Oh, this won't make any difference to my commission?
Nigel No.
Turner (*considering*) Still, better get something in writing. Good luck, Nigel.

He exits into the hall

Nigel takes the cases to the door, stops and listens

There is the faint sound of a Gregorian chant. It fades away

Nigel squares his shoulders and switches on the outside light. He opens the door

The sound of the Gregorian chant returns, this time with loud intensity

A cowled figure appears suddenly, framed in the doorway

(*Falling back in panic*) Oh bugger and bollocks — you've come for me.

Potter enters and switches on the main light. He is wearing a dark duffle coat. He drops the hood

Potter (*politely*) Well, yes, I have as a matter of fact, Mr Burke. I hope I didn't frighten you.

Nigel You scared the crap out of me.

Potter I came earlier but you were otherwise engaged ... upstairs. So I left the skull goblet in the hope that you'd reconsider.

Nigel Reconsider?

Potter Buying it.

Nigel But you were going to bury it at Newstead.

Potter (*shaking his head*) No.

Nigel No.

Potter I intended to keep the goblet for myself.

Nigel But why?

Potter To see what you saw, Mr Burke. You don't know how I envied you that. From the moment you told me I began to dream of repossessing the goblet — and drinking from it — and seeing Byron.

Nigel And did you?

Potter I drank from it but I didn't see him.

Nigel Why did you want to see him, Mr Potter?

Potter You don't know what it's like to be a complete nonentity.

Nigel But you're not ——

Potter I am. A complete nonentity. Yesterday I stood at the meat counter in Sainsbury's whilst the girls served four people behind me. I was invisible to them, Mr Burke; so, unfortunately, was Byron to me. I drank from the skull every night. I read his poetry. I could recite "She walks in beauty like the night" backwards. But he never came.

Nigel Why did it mean so much?

Potter (*hesitating*) I thought the experience would change me. Set me apart. Even make me attractive to women. When I saw you in the churchyard ... and in here with them ...

Nigel What?

Potter I thought perhaps he could do the same for me. But nothing's going to do that. You may have noticed that I'm on the small side, Mr Burke.

Nigel No, not small, Mr Potter.

Potter (*angrily*) Not? Is there something wrong with your eyesight, Mr Burke? I suggest you fetch a tape measure. I am small. A few inches less I'd be a dwarf.

Nigel We could all say that. You're getting this out of ... (*lamely*) ... proportion.

Potter If I were to leave this room now, how would you describe me? (*He passes deliberately behind Nigel*) The colour of my eyes, my hair? Do you remember them? Quickly — describe me.

Nigel Well, I'd have to say ...

Potter Small!

Nigel Mr Potter, all women aren't like that. I have a friend who'd refer to you as vertically challenged. After all, the limp made Byron ... and look at Napoleon.

Potter Don't ask me to look at Napoleon. His mother never called him Shorty.

Nigel Well, you may be small but you don't lack courage. You're not afraid of "the other one". I am.

Potter Ah. I have a confession to make there. I owe you that much peace of mind. There is no "other one". I made the story up to frighten you — to retrieve the skull goblet.

Nigel What? So he didn't frighten Arnold Fisher to death?

Potter There was no Arnold Fisher either and no family. How I came by the goblet is my affair but I did need a plausible, not to say tantalizing, story ...

Nigel But I've seen them. I saw the dog. I saw Byron. I've heard the chanting.

Potter Yes, and one day no doubt you'll see a mad monk but no one else will. And what do we deduce from that, Mr Burke? You're off your trolley.

Nigel Off my trolley. (*Grimly*) I see you've studied psychiatry, Potter.

Potter I'm sorry. I shouldn't have said that. But you are having a nervous breakdown. And so shall I if I don't get away. I must get away before I murder the old bat. Will you buy the goblet?

There is the distant sound of car horn

Nigel Mr Potter, as you can see, I'm leaving. I've no further use for the goblet. (*He moves to the door*)

Potter But I must have money. I have to get to Italy.

Nigel (*hesitating*) Why Italy?

Potter Because Byron went there. I thought it might change me. Give me a finish. Perhaps things would be different there. Perhaps people wouldn't look down on me.

Nigel (*helpfully*) Perhaps Japan would have been a better choice.

Potter gives him a sharp glance

Sorry.

Potter There was another reason. There was this article I read in a magazine.

The writer said she could never love a man who hadn't wandered through the goldsmiths' shops on the Ponte Vecchio ... or sipped Frascati within sight of the Spanish Steps ... or taken coffee by the Grand Canal ...

Nigel (*disgustedly*) What a naff thing to say. What a pseud. I don't believe it.

Potter It's true. It was in the series "My Favourite Places" by Julia Phillips.

Nigel (*staring*) Julia?

Potter Phillips. Don't you believe me?

Nigel (*after a pause*) Yes. It does sound the sort of thing she'd say.

Julia bursts into the room

Julia Are you coming, Nigel?

Nigel I was just saying goodbye to Mr ... er ——

Potter Potter.

Nigel Potter ... (*He gestures toward Potter*)

Julia (*ignoring Potter*) Where's Mary?

Nigel I think she's in the kitchen. May I introduce you to ——

Julia Have you told her?

Nigel Not in as many words.

Julia Not in as many words! What does that mean? Has she read the note?

Nigel Yes, but she didn't seem to understand it. Julia, I'd like you to meet ——

Julia Didn't understand it? This is impossible. Are you coming?

Nigel (*slowly*) Julia, I've been thinking. Perhaps you're right. Perhaps it would be better if you had it out with her.

Julia (*hesitating*) Do you think so?

Nigel Try to make her understand. Clear the air. Wipe the slate clean.

Julia It would be the civilized thing. In the kitchen?

Nigel Yes.

Julia Are you coming?

Nigel No, I'll stay here with Mr ... er —— (*He gestures towards Potter*)

Julia I won't be long.

She exits through the hall door

Potter Now do you see the extent of the problem? Totally invisible. Will you help me to get to Italy?

Nigel (*decisively*) I'll do more than that. I'll come with you.

Potter What about the lady?

Nigel Never mind the lady.

There is the sound of Julia's and Mary's raised voices from the kitchen. Nigel takes his passport from the desk

Here's my passport.

Potter Passport. But you're an agoraphobic. What are you doing with a passport?

Nigel Even agoraphobics can dream, Potter. Is it in order?

Potter Yes. There's nothing in it.

Nigel Then it's time there was.

Potter But what about money?

Nigel Can you use a cash dispenser? Can you enter a bank without having an asthma attack even though you have a full account?

Potter Yes, but I haven't got a full account.

Nigel That's all right. I can get it in if you can get it out.

Potter (*smiling*) I'll take your cases, Mr Burke. My car's outside.

Nigel Oh, I must warn you. I have a fear of flying. I'm nervous of strangers — and I may have hysterics in the airport.

Potter picks up the cases, moves to the door and stops

Potter Then why come?

There is the sound of a crash from the kitchen

Nigel (*smiling*) I think it's what they call flooding, Mr Potter. I'll join you in the car. I just have to say goodbye to someone.

Potter Right. And don't worry, Mr Burke. We'll get by. I do know a little Italian ...

Nigel Ah, so that's why you want to go to Italy. You know a little Italian.

Potter (*with a thin smile*) I suppose I will get used to your sense of humour, Mr Burke ... in time.

Potter exits with the cases

Nigel (*taking a last look around the study at the bust and the portraits*) Well, it's my turn to say goodbye now, George. I didn't mean the things I said. I don't know if you're a ghost or a nervous breakdown but I'm going to trust Byron. I shall probably regret it — most people did. (*He moves to the door and then turns*) Oh, one other thing: about your funeral. I didn't tell you the whole of it. When they brought you back to Nottingham, the workers and the lacemakers of the city hadn't forgotten your defence of their liberties. They followed your coffin in solemn procession half a mile long from Nottingham to Hucknall St Mary's. And when someone asked why they mourned the bad Lord Byron they said, "He was such a great man we've forgotten his faults." Just thought I'd mention that. (*He begins putting on the hat and scarf, stops, changes his mind and throws them away. He opens the door*)

Byron (*voice over*) Go on, Nigel — you can do it.

  Nigel exits

There are further raised voices in the kitchen

  Turner backs into the room from the hall. He blows out his cheeks and looks around for something to drink

There is a further crash from the kitchen

  Turner picks up the skull goblet and drains it. He realizes what he's done and shudders. He crosses back to the hall door to listen

The executive chair turns around and faces the window

There is a creaking sound that grows louder and louder and the back of the chair swings from side to side. Turner hears the sound and turns slowly, seeing the chair moving. He stares

The motion grows faster and faster

Black-out

CURTAIN

FURNITURE AND PROPERTY LIST

ACT I
SCENE 1

On stage: Large desk. *On it*: papers, scripts, pens etc., bust of Byron, torch, glass
                 of red wine, bottle of red wine, other glasses. *In drawer*: passport
                 Executive chair
                 Easy chairs, sofa
                 Coloured metal balls for **Nigel**
                 Walking stick

Off stage: Harrods bag containing skull goblet (**Potter**)
                 Playscript (**Julia**)

Personal: **Julia**: watch (worn throughout)

SCENE 2

Re-set: Executive chair facing window

Set: New bottle of wine if necessary

Strike: **Julia**'s playscript
                 Wine bottle from ACT I SCENE 1 if necessary

Off stage: Dog-eared duplicate of **Julia**'s script (**Nigel**)
                 Script

ACT II
SCENE 1

Re-set: Coloured metal balls in desk drawer

Off stage: Playscript (**Turner**)
                 Bag containing soft hat, scarf, heavy glasses, newspaper (**Julia**)

SCENE 2

Re-set: Executive chair facing window

Set: Harrods bag containing skull goblet behind sofa cushion

Off stage: Two suitcases (**Nigel**)

LIGHTING PLOT

One interior setting with exterior backing
Practical fittings required: table lamp, garden light

ACT I, SCENE 1

To open: General interior lighting on study: darkness outside windows

Cue 1	**Nigel** switches off the light *Dim interior lighting*	(Page 13)
Cue 2	A rush of air: **Nigel** turns *Bring up bright white light on* **Byron**	(Page 13)
Cue 3	**Nigel** falls back in horror *Black-out*	(Page 13)

ACT I, SCENE 2

To open: As opening of ACT I SCENE 1

No cues

ACT II, SCENE 1

To open: As opening of ACT I SCENE 2

Cue 4	**Byron**: " ... can't be Byron just by limping ... " *Black-out; bring lights up again when ready*	(Page 37)
Cue 5	**Nigel** switches off room lights *Snap to dim interior light*	(Page 42)
Cue 6	**Nigel** switches on garden light *Bring up bright light on exterior backing*	(Page 42)
Cue 7	**Mary** switches on interior lights *Snap up interior lights*	(Page 42)

ACT II, SCENE 2

To open: Dim early morning exterior light; table lamp on

Cue 8	Rush of air and tinkling sounds *Black-out: return to previous setting when ready*	(Page 49)
Cue 9	**Byron**: " —— and we have to face him alone ..." *Begin to fade lights*	(Page 50)
Cue 10	**Nigel**: " ... a pain in the arse as well." *Brighten lights*	(Page 50)
Cue 11	**Nigel**: "And if I wasn't an agoraphobic I'd come ... " *Black-out*	(Page 50)
Cue 12	**Nigel**: "No George, don't go. I didn't mean ... " *Black-out*	(Page 51)
Cue 13	**Nigel** switches on garden light *Bring up bright light on exterior backing*	(Page 51)
Cue 14	**Potter** switches on main light *Bring up general interior lighting on study*	(Page 52)

EFFECTS PLOT

ACT I

Cue 1	**Nigel**: " ... an improvement on this ... " *Low whining of a dog*	(Page 1)
Cue 2	**Nigel** peers out and shines the torch *Whining turns into a growl*	(Page 1)
Cue 3	**Nigel**: " ... who looks like her father —— " *Doorbell*	(Page 5)
Cue 4	**Nigel** opens the hall door *Faint tinkling sound; rush of air sound*	(Page 13)
Cue 5	**Byron** exits into the garden *Rush of air sound*	(Page 23)

ACT II

Cue 6	**Byron**: " ... can't be Byron just by limping ..." *Rush of air*	(Page 37)
Cue 7	**Nigel** unbolts the door *Gregorian chant*	(Page 42)
Cue 8	**Nigel** listens harder *Fade Gregorian chant*	(Page 42)
Cue 9	**Nigel** opens the door *Gregorian chant again, rising in volume*	(Page 42)
Cue 10	**Mary** enters *Cut Gregorian chant*	(Page 42)
Cue 11	**Nigel** returns to his note *Squeal of brakes*	(Page 46)
Cue 12	**Nigel**: " ... supposed to be buried at Newstead." *Rush of air, tinkling sound*	(Page 49)

Cue 13	Lights come up to previous setting *Car horn*	(Page 51)
Cue 14	**Nigel** takes the cases to the door and stops *Faint Gregorian chant; fade after a moment*	(Page 51)
Cue 15	**Nigel** opens the door *Loud, intense Gregorian chant*	(Page 51)
Cue 16	**Potter**: "Will you buy the goblet?" *Car horn*	(Page 53)
Cue 17	**Potter**: "Then why come?" *Crash from kitchen*	(Page 55)
Cue 18	**Nigel** opens the door **Byron**'s *voice-over as script p. 56*	(Page 55)
Cue 19	**Turner** looks for something to drink *Further crash from kitchen*	(Page 56)
Cue 20	**Turner** listens at the hall door *Creaking sound, growing louder and louder*	(Page 56)